DISCARD

Materials

Plastic

By Rhonda Donald Lucas

Consultant:
Marjorie Weiner
Assistant Director
National Plastics Center & Museum
Leominster, Massachusetts

Capstone *press*
Mankato, Minnesota

First Facts is published by Capstone Press
151 Good Counsel Drive, P.O. Box 669, Mankato, Minnesota 56002
www.capstonepress.com

Library of Congress Cataloging-in-Publication Data
Lucas, Rhonda Donald.
    Plastic / Rhonda Donald Lucas.
    p. cm. — (First facts. Materials)
    Includes bibliographical references and index.
    Contents: Plastic—What is plastic?—Natural polymers—How plastic is made—From
cars to clothing—Different plastics for Different Uses—What plastic can do—Recycling
plastic—Amazing but true!—Hands on: make poly putty.
    ISBN 0-7368-2514-2 (hardcover)
    1. Plastics—Juvenile literature. [1. Plastics.] I. Title. II. Series.
TP1120.L84 2004
620.1'923—dc22   2003015050

Credits
Heather Adamson and Blake A. Hoena, editors; Jennifer Bergstrom, series designer; Wanda
    Winch and Deirdre Barton, photo researchers; Gary Sundermeyer, photographer; Eric
    Kudalis, product planning editor

Photo credits
Capstone Press/Gary Sundermeyer, cover, 1, 5, 6–7, 13, 14–15, 16, 17, 19
Corbis/Ecoscene/Alan Towse, 11; Peter Yates, 12
Corel, 8, 9
NASA, 20

The author wishes to thank Rob Krebs from the American Plastics Council for his help in
researching this book.

1 2 3 4 5 6 09 08 07 06 05 04

Table of Contents

Plastic

Paco sets his helmet on the counter and then takes off his sunglasses. He pours a cup of milk from a milk jug. He peels off the wrapper of a snack bar. Paco puts a disc into his CD player. People use many items made out of plastic.

What Is Plastic?

Plastics are human-made **polymers**. Polymers are tiny pieces of matter that are linked together. Under a microscope, they look like a chain of paper clips. People make plastics that can be hard, silky, stretchy, or bouncy.

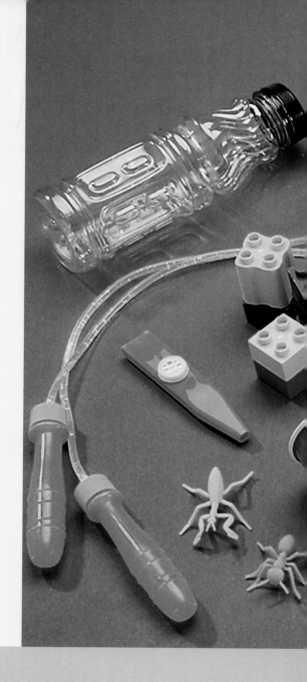

 Fun Fact:
The first moldable plastic was made in 1868. Billiard balls were the first objects made out of this plastic.

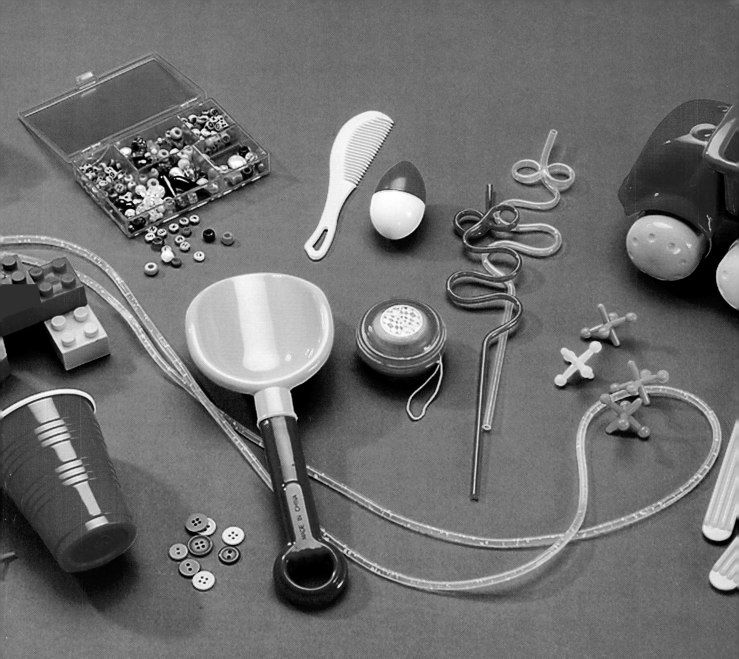

Natural Polymers

The idea for plastic came from nature. Fingernails, horns, and skin are **natural** polymers. People saw that polymers could be strong like a turtle shell.

People wanted human-made polymers
to be like natural polymers. They invented
plastics that were strong or soft. Polymers
also could be stretchy like a spider web.

 fun fact:
A thread of spider silk is stronger than the same
size thread of steel. Spider silk also stretches.

How Plastic Is Made

When oil and gas are **refined**, a leftover product called **resin** is made. Machines called converters heat the resin and other materials to more than 1,000 degrees Fahrenheit (538 degrees Celsius). The materials are turned into plastic powder, flakes, or small seed-sized pellets.

From Cars to Clothing

Plastic powders, flakes, and pellets are made into many products. They can be melted and pushed into **molds**. Car bumpers and toys are made from molded plastic.

Melted plastic also can be spun into threads. The threads are woven to make cloth. Scarves, shirts, sweaters, carpet, and backpacks can be made from plastic.

Different Plastics for Different Uses

Plastics have many uses. Plastic bends in a child's jump rope. Clear plastic is used for windows and lenses in eyeglasses. The plastic in diapers is soft and absorbent.

Fun Fact:
"Thirsty" plastics can absorb up to 600 times their weight in water. These plastics are used in products such as diapers.

What Plastic Can Do

Plastics are light, strong, and last a long time. A heavy glass jar breaks if it is dropped. A light plastic jar will not shatter if it falls.

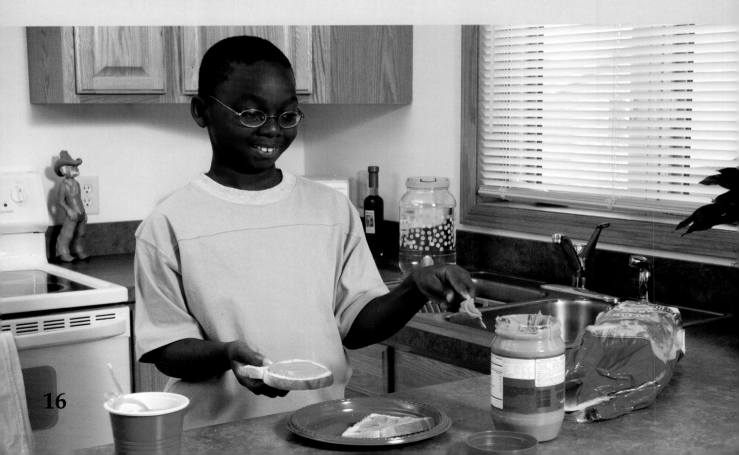

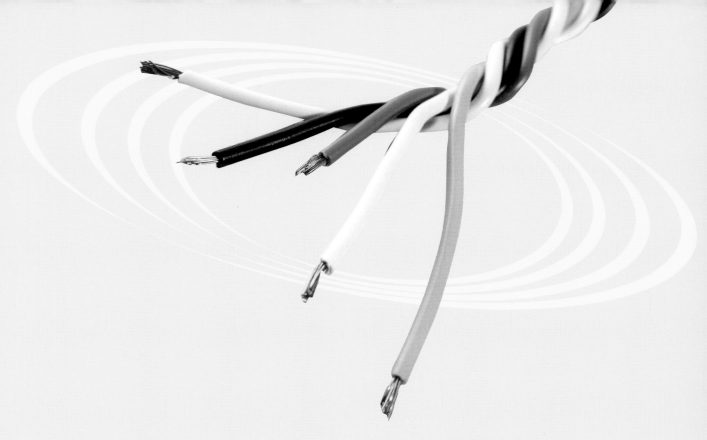

Some plastics are **insulators**. They keep **electricity** safe inside wires. People do not get a shock when they touch the plastic covering the wires.

Recycling Plastic

Plastic takes up a lot of space in landfills, but used plastics can be recycled. They can be made into other things. Milk jugs can be made into park benches. Soda bottles can be turned into sweatshirts or carpet. Companies also try to make plastics that create less waste.

Astronauts on the International Space Station may soon live in thin plastic rooms. The rooms would blow up like giant balloons. The inflatable rooms would be easy to pack and carry into space. Astronauts could sleep and work inside the rooms.

Hands On: Make Poly Putty

See how plastic can be stretchy and bouncy by making a polymer of your own.

What You Need

1 cup (240 mL) warm water
1 teaspoon (5 mL) borax powder (available in the laundry
    section of stores)
¼ cup (60 mL) white glue (not washable or school glue)
¼ cup (60 mL) cold water
measuring cup
measuring spoon
small bowl
spoon
air-tight container

What You Do

1. Put warm water in measuring cup. Stir in borax powder
   until it disappears. Set aside.
2. Mix glue and cold water in small bowl. Add 3 teaspoons
   (15 mL) of the borax mixture. Stir until mixture forms a blob.
3. Squeeze the blob in your hands until it is smooth and no
   longer sticky.
4. Try stretching the putty into different shapes. Roll it into a
   ball and bounce it. Keep your putty in an air-tight container.

Glossary

electricity (ih-lek-TRISS-uh-tee)—a form of energy used to run machines or produce heat and light

insulator (IN-suh-late-ur)—a material that keeps electricity inside wires or paths

mold (MOLD)—a shaped container

natural (NACH-ur-uhl)—found in or produced by nature

polymer (POL-uh-mur)—tiny pieces of matter that are linked together; there are natural polymers and human-made polymers

refine (ri-FINE)—to remove unwanted matter from oil or gas

resin (REZ-in)—a semisolid substance that is made when oil and gas are refined; the resin is used to make plastics.

Read More

Llewellyn, Claire. *Plastic.* Material World. New York: Franklin Watts, 2002.

Oxlade, Chris. *Plastic.* Materials, Materials, Materials. Chicago: Heinemann, 2001.

Internet Sites

FactHound offers a safe, fun way to find Internet sites related to this book. All of the sites on FactHound have been researched by our staff.

Here's how:
1. Visit *www.facthound.com*
2. Type in this special code **0736825142** for age-appropriate sites. Or enter a search word related to this book for a more general search.
3. Click on the Fetch It button.

FactHound will fetch the best sites for you!

Index